Yoga

Elizabeth Silas and Diane Goodney

Franklin Watts
A Division of Scholastic Inc.
New York • Toronto • London • Auckland • Sydney
Mexico City • New Delhi • Hong Kong
Danbury, Connecticut

Dedication
We dedicate this book to all our teachers—past, present, and future—and to all our students. Lokah samastah sukhino bhavantu.

IMPORTANT: Not all exercises are suitable for everyone, and this or any exercise program may result in injury. Any user of this book assumes the risk of injury resulting from performing the exercises. To reduce risk of injury, consult your doctor before beginning any exercise program. The instructions and advice presented are in no way intended as a substitute for medical counseling. The authors, publishers, and distributors of this book disclaim any liabilities or loss in connection with the exercises and advice herein.

Cover illustration by Peter Cho.
Cover and interior design by Kathleen Santini.
Illustrations by Pat Rasch.

Library of Congress Cataloging-in-Publication Data

Silas, Elizabeth.
  Yoga: life balance / Elizabeth Silas and Diane Goodney.
      p. cm.
Includes bibliographical references and index.
Contents: What is Yoga?—Yoga ways of living: yama and niyama—Yoga movement and breath (asana and pranayama)—Yoga stillness: pratyahara, dharana, dhyana, samadhi.
  ISBN 0-531-12258-1 (lib. bdg.)   0-531-15577-3 (pbk.)
  1. Yoga—Juvenile literature. 2. Ashtanga yoga—Juvenile literature.
[1. Yoga.] I. Goodney, Diane. II. Title.
  RA781.7.S54 2003
  613.7'046—dc21
                                        2003000108

Table of Contents

A Note to the Reader

In the next four chapters you will learn a lot about the practice of yoga. You may decide that you want to try it yourself. If you do, make sure you ask your parents first, and ask them to check with your doctor before you start to practice yoga postures regularly. If you have heart problems, breathing problems (such as asthma), an injury, or other medical conditions, there may be some postures that will make your condition worse.

In addition, if you ever try a yoga posture or exercise and you feel pain, carefully come out of the position and rest. Do not continue any activity that causes you pain. Remember—the most important thing about yoga is learning to become aware of your breath and your movements, not learning to bend or stretch really far.

If you do not feel well for any reason, do not practice yoga until you feel better. Yoga can be helpful for some illnesses and conditions, but you need to work with a qualified teacher. You should not practice when you are feeling tired, weak, or sick.

This book is a basic introduction to yoga. It is best to learn yoga practices from a qualified yoga teacher. A teacher can help you practice postures safely, recommend postures that are best for you personally, and inspire you to practice with dedication. However, this book can teach you about where yoga came from and how it is practiced by many people today.

One

What Is Yoga?

Have you ever had such a good day that you wish you could remember every detail about it, or a really bad day, when it felt like nothing went right? Practicing yoga gives you a way to handle these situations, and many more.

Many people think that yoga is just people bending their bodies into all kinds of strange positions. In fact, that's just one part of yoga. Yoga is actually a way of living. It is a set of techniques that helps you take care of your body, think more clearly, and really pay attention to what you are doing at every moment. When you have a wonderful day, your mind will be clear enough to remember all the details. If you have a horrible day, you will be able to make the best of the problems that come up. Yoga helps you to unite your body, mind, and spirit, so that you can be the best person you can be.

Where Does Yoga Come From?

Yoga is very old. It originated thousands of years ago in India. Because the Buddhist philosophy and the Hindu religion also have their roots in India, people sometimes associate them with yoga. But yoga is an independent tradition. The techniques are not tied to any one religion or culture—anyone can practice yoga.

Because yoga has developed over so many years, various techniques have been tried. These became the different "paths" of yoga, or the different ways that you can learn and practice yoga. In this way, yoga is not like a sport. Baseball, for example, has rules; no matter where you play it, the rules are the same. Learning yoga is more like learning to build a house. If you learn to build a house in West Africa, you may learn to build it in a different way than you would in Norway. Some of the building techniques will be the same, while others will be different. In both cases, you learn to build something you can live in.

Similarly, you can learn different types of yoga, with different techniques, from different teachers and books. Although some techniques will be the same, others will be different. In all cases, you learn to take care of your mind and body.

The Eight Parts of Yoga

About two thousand years ago, a wise man named Patanjali wrote the *Yoga Sutras*. The *Yoga Sutras* were written in Sanskrit, an ancient language. They describe eight "limbs" of yoga. Like the limbs of a tree, these limbs are all connected. Each represents things you can do to become more aware of yourself and the world. The eight limbs in Sanskrit are *yama, niyama, asana, pranayama, pratyahara, dharana, dhyana,* and *samadhi*.

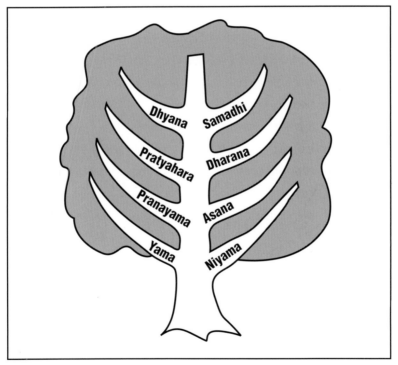

The eight limbs of the "tree" of yoga.

Yama and niyama are guidelines for how to live and act—the do's and don'ts of life. Asanas are the physical positions that most people think of when they hear the word *yoga*. Pranayama is conscious breathing. Asana and pranayama usually go hand in hand, because they are the physical activities that help bring your mind and body into harmony. They require a lot of energy and focus.

What Does Yoga Mean?

Sanskrit may look strange, but it comes from the same ancient language as English. The Sanskrit word yoga comes from the same root as the English word yoke. When you yoke two horses together, you unite them so they will combine their strength and work. In the same way, when you practice yoga you unite all the different parts of yourself: your thoughts, emotions, and physical sensations. When you practice yoga regularly, you begin to feel more united with everyone and everything else in the world.

The last four limbs are spiritual ones. They are gradual steps to complete meditation. Pratyahara is withdrawing the senses from the outside world. Dharana is concentrating on one thing or idea completely. These two steps can be practiced together with exercises that help clear the mind. When people practice these two steps regularly, they often feel refreshed and energized afterward. They have taken a break from all the noise of everyday life—the television flickering, the phone ringing, and people asking them to do things.

Once you have mastered pratyahara and dharana the next step is dhyana. Dhyana occurs when you concentrate completely on one thing for an extended period of time. This is called meditation. Finally, samadhi is often described as complete bliss, the greatest joy.

Patanjali's eight-limbed path is only one of many paths of yoga. It is often called ashtanga yoga, raja yoga, or classical yoga, and it is the path we will explore in this book. (If you are interested in the other paths, check out some of the books in the Further Resources section in the back of this book.)

Patanjali did not invent these practices; people were using them long before he wrote them down. Today's yoga teachers have taken something thousands of years old and made it useful in modern life. Millions of people around the world practice yoga today because of the many benefits it offers.

The Benefits of Practicing Yoga

People practice yoga for many different reasons. Practicing the postures helps to keep your body fit. Although you may already be developing muscular strength and cardiovascular endurance through sports, weight training, or dance, many of these fitness activities do not build flexibility of the spine, back, arms, and legs. Yoga postures help you gain flexibility *and* strength, which helps to prevent injuries.

Yoga can help you feel better in your everyday activities. For example, you may spend most of the day sitting—at your desk, in front of a computer or television, and at the dinner table. This can make you stiff and uncomfortable. Practicing yoga helps your body endure these long sitting spells, and it teaches you how to sit and stand properly to keep from getting aches.

Practicing yoga postures also helps your body to balance its hormones. Hormones are chemicals produced by one part of the body, released into the bloodstream, and carried to "target cells" in other parts of the body that need them to function. Your body grows and changes when hormones are at work. Yoga postures can help you feel better in physical ways (for example, girls often find that they have less cramping during their menstrual periods). They can also help you feel better in emotional ways (for example, some people find that they are less likely to get into fights over things they don't really care about). This link between your physical body and your emotions is hard to explain, but many people experience it.

Not only is your body growing; your mind is also developing. Focusing on yoga for a few minutes each day clears your mind of all the things other people tell you—

input from your friends, your coach, your parents, television shows, and magazine ads. It lets you focus on what's going on inside *you* for a little while. As you practice, yoga will increase your ability to look within, think for yourself, and trust yourself.

Focusing on yoga for a few minutes each day clears your mind of all the things other people tell you—input from your friends, your coach, your parents, television shows, and magazine ads.

At a time when everything in your life is changing so quickly, practicing yoga regularly can make you feel more self-confident and see things in a more positive way. It helps you accept and understand yourself. It's easy to grow up wearing "masks" that cover up who you really are. Yoga helps you take off masks, so that you can show everyone your true self.

Yoga is all this, but the best thing is… it's fun! There's always something new: a new posture to practice or a new way to think about breathing. You may see dramatic changes, such as doing a handstand for the first time, or small changes, such as being able to balance a little longer on one foot. As you grow older you may practice yoga for different reasons, but if you keep practicing, you can continue to learn new things about yourself and have fun doing it.

Yoga Movement and Breath

The physical exercises of yoga are called asana, or postures. Postures are more than stretches or gymnastic exercises. When we stretch, we may think about our day or even hold a conversation. When we practice gymnastics, we work on the final "look" of a routine, striving to perfect the movement. When we practice yoga postures, we focus all our attention on our body and breath, noticing what we are feeling in each posture. The goal of practicing asana is not to perfect the postures, but to get to know your body and to focus your mind.

When to Practice

Try to practice yoga postures every day, whether it is for ten minutes, twenty minutes, or sixty minutes. Regular practice is the key. You will feel best when you do yoga postures every day—even if you only do a few. To make the most of your practice:

- Set aside a time when no one will interrupt you and you will not have to rush.
- Practice yoga on a near-empty stomach. Wait two to three hours after a large meal and one to two hours after a light meal or snack.
- Drink plenty of water *before* you practice so you don't become dehydrated.

Where to Practice

It's great to have a special place to practice. Make it some-place you enjoy being so you'll look forward to going to your very own yoga area. Here's what you need:

- You need a clear space with no furniture. The room should be warm, not cold or hot. (If you practice outside, practice in the shade.)
- The floor must be flat, level, and smooth. Make sure there is nothing that can hurt your bare feet.
- Turn off the radio and television. Close the door to keep pets and siblings out.

How to Practice

You want to be as comfortable as possible when you practice so you can focus on what you're doing.

- Practice in bare feet. This will help you keep your feet in place and stop them from slipping. It will also help you become aware of how your feet connect with the floor and the earth.
- Wear clothing that you can move freely in. It should not stop your movements. Shorts and a T-shirt are fine, as long as the shorts are somewhat stretchy or loose. Leggings and tank tops work well, too.
- If your hair is long, tie it back.
- A "sticky mat" is very helpful. It helps your feet and hands "stick" in place instead of slipping around. It also provides some cushioning when you are kneeling, sitting, and lying down. You can buy a sticky mat at a yoga studio or a sporting-goods store, or order one from the Internet.

Getting Started

Look at your yoga practice as an ongoing process rather than a goal-oriented one. No matter which posture you practice or how far "into" the posture you go, you are gaining the benefits of yoga practice if you focus on what you're doing. You can also reflect on your attitude before you start to practice each day. Ask yourself why you are practicing. Notice how your mind-set will have a great effect on your practice.

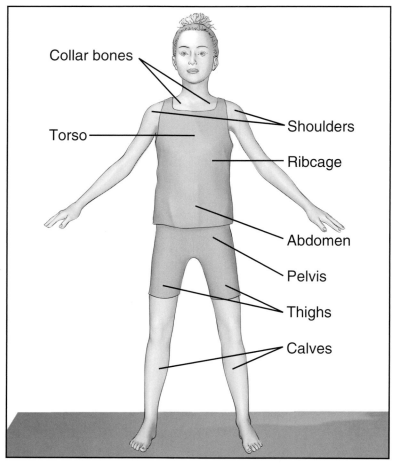

While practicing yoga, you may become aware of parts of your body you never noticed before.

A famous yoga teacher, K. Pattabhi Jois, says, "Yoga is ninety-nine percent practice and one percent theory." No matter how much of this book you read, if you don't start practicing, you'll never experience what yoga can do for you. So let's try some postures.

Mountain (Tadasana)

Mountain may seem very easy at first, but most of us don't balance our weight evenly when we stand; we tend to slump. Mountain will teach you to balance. As your spine lifts and your shoulders relax back you will look taller and feel more confident. Imagine yourself standing as tall and majestic as a mountain. ** NOTE: Throughout this book we will be describing how to breathe. "Inhale" means "breathe in." "Exhale" means "breathe out."

1. Start by bringing the feet together. Let the big toes touch and the heels stay just slightly apart. Distribute your weight evenly on your feet.
2. Rock forward onto the balls of your feet and backward onto your heels. Make smaller and smaller rocking movements until you feel perfectly balanced between the balls and the heels of your feet. Then do the same with the inside and outside edges of your feet.

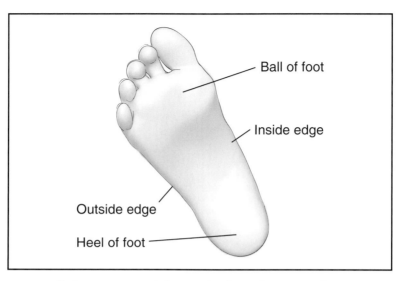

Balance your weight evenly throughout your feet.

3. Lift your toes and spread them apart. Then place them back down on the floor.

4. Exhale. Press into the floor with both feet, using your leg muscles. As you gently squeeze, or contract, your thigh muscles, feel your kneecaps lift up.

5. Inhale. Pull your belly in gently. Lengthen your entire spine from the tip of your tailbone to your head, lifting the top of your head toward the sky.

6. Exhale. Lift your shoulders up and gently roll them back so your chest lifts up and forward. Reach your fingertips toward the floor.

7. Hold the posture for five breaths. Look straight ahead,

but don't look at anything in particular. Just gaze. (If this is difficult for you, close your eyes.) Feel each exhalation pressing your feet into the ground, allowing you to stand firmly, as solid as a mountain. Feel each inhalation making you taller, like a mountain reaching to the sky.

Sun Salutation A (Suryanamaskara A)

The Sun Salutation warms up the body and the breath at the beginning of a yoga practice. It is a series of postures linked together by movements and the breath. The Sun Salutation allows you to stretch and strengthen the entire body, and it is a wonderful way to learn to coordinate your breath and your movements.

1. Start from Mountain and focus on your breath. Inhale, raising your arms out to the sides and then all the way overhead until the palms touch.

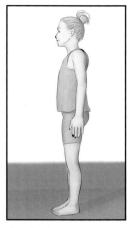

Each time you practice yoga postures, begin in Mountain.

Inhale as you raise your arms overhead.

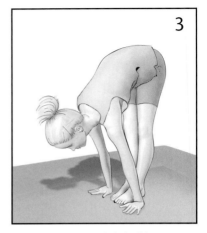

Exhale as you fold forward.   *Inhale as you lift halfway up.*

2. Exhale and bend forward, reaching your arms out to the sides and all the way down until the fingertips (eventually the palms) touch the floor. Keep your lower belly pulling inward.

3. Inhale and lift halfway up while keeping your fingertips on the floor, until your spine feels long and straight.

4. Exhale. Place your palms on the floor, right underneath your shoulders. Step or jump softly back into a "plank" position, with your body in a straight line (like a plank of wood). Make sure your feet land hip-distance apart and drop your knees to the floor. Bend your elbows, keeping them close to the sides of your body, and lower your chest until it is three inches from the floor. (Once your arms are stronger, you can keep your knees off the floor and lower

down into a full "yoga push-up.") Keep your belly pulled in, your elbows close to your ribs, and your shoulders lifted away from the ground.

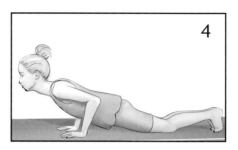

Exhale as you step back to this position.

5. Inhale. Press your chest forward and up toward the sky as you roll forward onto the tops of your feet. Your hands press into the floor as your arms straighten. The chest lifts up and forward. The shoulders lift up and back.

Inhale as you roll forward and lift your chest.

6. Exhale. Lift your hips up toward the sky as you roll back onto the balls and toes of your feet. Bring your body into an upside-down V. Take five breaths as you hold this posture,

Exhale as you lift your hips into an upside-down V shape.

called the Downward-Facing Dog. Make sure your hands are shoulder-distance apart and your feet are hip-distance apart. Look toward your knees. As you inhale, lift the sitting bones toward the sky. As you exhale, press the heels toward the ground.

7. Inhale. Step or jump forward softly, placing your feet between your hands. Then extend your spine long and straight.

8. Exhale and bend forward, reaching your fingertips (and eventually your palms) to the floor.

9. Inhale as you reach your arms out to the sides and then up overhead until your palms touch.

10. Exhale. Sweep your arms down to your sides, back to Mountain.

Inhale as you step forward and lift halfway up.

Exhale as you fold forward.

Inhale as you raise your arms overhead.

Make your movement and breath flow smoothly, remembering that the movement between postures is just as important as the postures themselves. Make each movement last as long as your inhalation or exhalation takes. This will take practice. Don't ever hold your breath! If you start to feel as though you're panting or it's hard to breathe, take a rest in Mountain or sit down.

Your Sun Salutation will change over time. When you start practicing, it will feel and look one way. After a month or two of regular practice, it will feel and look very different. (In fact, this is true of all the postures.)

Here Comes the Sun

In some ancient cultures people would begin their day by welcoming the sun as it appeared on the horizon. People saw the sun as an awesome source of light and energy, and considered it a symbol of the light and energy they carried within themselves. By showing respect to the sun, they were showing respect for the source of life inside themselves and in all beings. Practicing the Sun Salutation first thing in the morning, yogis (people who practice yoga) faced the sun as it rose in the east. This is how the front of the body became known as the east side, while the back of the body became known as the west side.

Breathe Easy

Breathing is an important part of practicing the yoga postures. Focusing on proper breathing will help you move into and out of the postures smoothly, and can even help you hold postures more steadily. Rather than using force to get into or hold a posture, you can use your breath to help you ease gently into the posture when you are ready. Try to follow these basic guidelines as you practice:

- Breathe through the nose, keeping the mouth closed.
- Take full breaths. Maintain this full breathing throughout each movement and posture. (If your breathing becomes fast or shallow, stop to rest.)
- When you start an inhalation or exhalation, start your movement. As you end the inhalation or exhalation, finish the movement. Then go right into the next. Don't ever hold your breath.

In general, we exhale during movements that "close" the front of the body or move downward. These are movements such as lowering the arms, bending forward, bending to the side, twisting, and coming down from a backward bend. We inhale during movements that "open" the front of the body or move upward. These are actions such as raising the arms; coming up out of a forward bend, a side bend, or a twist; and bending backward.

There are different ways of breathing that are meant to help your body in special ways. For example, some people practice ujjayi breathing while in postures. Ujjayi is a way of breathing so that you can hear your breath as it moves through your throat. Ujjayi breathing should be learned from a yoga teacher after you have been practicing for a while. When you first learn the postures, you don't need to use ujjayi; just use the rules for breathing outlined on the previous page.

Warrior A (Virabhadrasana A)

Practicing Warrior A strengthens your legs, back, and abdominal muscles, and it helps relieve stiffness in your shoulders and neck. Imagine taking on the strength and energy of a warrior as you practice this posture.

1. Begin in Mountain. Inhale and jump your feet wide apart. Place your hands on your hips.

2. Exhale. Point both your feet to the left. At the same time, turn your torso to the left, so that your chest and your hips are facing the same direction as your left toes.

3. Inhale and raise your arms overhead, hands shoulder-distance apart with palms facing in.

4. Exhale. Bend your left knee until your left thigh is parallel to the floor. Turn your gaze upward, past your thumbs.

5. Take five breaths, and hold the posture. Your right leg is straight and strong. Reach upward through your torso and arms.

6. Inhale, then straighten your left leg, keeping your arms raised.

7. Exhale and turn your feet so they both point to the right. Bend your right knee and turn your chest and

Press your shoulders down, away from your ears.

hips to face the right.

8. Take five breaths and hold the posture on this side.

9. Inhale and straighten your right leg.

10. Exhale. Jump back to Mountain.

Warrior B (Virabhadrasana B)

This posture promotes strength and endurance, like that of a warrior; but at the same time, it lets you feel more open. It will build muscle strength in your legs and arms.

1. Begin in Mountain. Inhale. Jump your feet wide apart. Raise your arms to shoulder height, and make sure your hands are directly over your feet. Your arms and fingers should be straight and stretching outward, with your palms facing the floor.

Keep your bent knee directly over your heel. Make sure you can see the big toe of that foot. Otherwise, you can hurt your knee.

2. Exhale as you point your left foot to the left and turn your right foot in slightly to the left. Bend your left knee until your left thigh is parallel to the floor. Keep your right leg straight and strong. Look out over your left hand.

3. Hold the posture, and take five breaths. Feel your energy reaching out in four directions: upward through the top of your head, downward through the base of your spine, out through the fingertips of your left hand, and out through the fingertips of your right hand. Imagine that you are being pulled in all these directions, yet you stand your ground by keeping your torso tall and strong.

4. Inhale. Straighten your left leg.

5. Exhale. Turn your feet to repeat the posture facing the right. Now your right knee is bent and your head is turned to the right. Look out over your right hand.

6. Hold the posture, and take five breaths. Be sure to keep your entire torso facing the side. Only the neck and head turn to face your hand at the front.

7. Inhale and straighten your right leg.

8. Exhale and jump back to Mountain.

Time-Out

Choose ten minutes every day that you can use to practice yoga. This may be right after your morning shower, or right after you get home from school. (Make sure it's not right after a meal or just before you go to bed.) Every day for ten days, use those ten minutes to practice five Sun Salutations. Then start to add other postures that are in this book. This will help you establish a regular routine, which you can add to when you have time.

Fierce Posture (Utkatasana)

This posture helps the legs and abdomen become strong and flexible. It can be a very "fierce" and intense position!

1. Begin in Mountain. Inhale. Bend your knees and lower your tailbone toward the floor as you sweep your arms above your head. Your arms are shoulder-distance apart, palms facing in. Look up between your hands. Your legs are touching at the knees, ankles, and toes.

To keep your back from arching too much, pull your belly in and up.

2. Hold the posture, and take five breaths. As you inhale, reach up through the top of your head and your fingers. As you exhale, pull your lower belly in and up.

3. Exhale and come back to Mountain.

Triangle (Utthita Trikonasana)

While forward bends and back bends focus on the abdominal and back muscles, it is important to keep the sides of your body stretched and toned as well. Practicing Triangle helps you do this by lengthening and twisting your sides.

1. Begin in Mountain. Inhale. Jump your feet wide apart.

2. Exhale as you point your right foot to the right and turn your left foot in slightly to the right.

3. Inhale. Raise your arms to shoulder height (in a T position), palms facing down, and make sure your wrists are directly over your feet. Your arms and fingers should be straight and stretching outward. Expand your chest, and lift your spine.

4. Exhale. Bend sideways to the right, and let your right hand rest lightly on your right shin. (At first, put your hand just below your knee. After you have practiced for a while, you can begin to place the hand closer to the foot.) Extend your left arm straight up toward the sky.

5. Hold the posture for five breaths. Lift your gaze upward, past your left hand. Keep your chest open.

6. Inhale as you slowly come up.

7. Exhale. Turn your feet to point your left foot to the left and your right foot slightly to the left.

8. Inhale. Keep your arms shoulder height (in a T position), palms facing down, stretching outward. Expand through your chest, and lift your spine.

Imagine a wall behind you. Press your shoulders and arms back against that imaginary wall. This will help keep you from leaning too far forward.

9. Exhale. Bend sideways to the left, and let your left hand rest lightly on your left shin. Extend your right arm straight up toward the sky.
10. Hold the posture on this side for five breaths. Take your gaze upward, past your right hand.
11. Inhale as you slowly come up.
12. Exhale to Mountain.

> ### Hold It!
> In the beginning, hold each posture for five breaths. Once you are familiar with the postures, you can practice each one longer, working up to eight or ten breaths. Count each breath so you know when to come out of the posture. Work on making each breath full and steady.

Half Moon (Ardha Chandrasana)

Half Moon can be a tricky balancing posture. Don't hold your breath in an attempt to hold this posture. Breathing will help you keep the center of your body strong, which will help you keep your balance.

1. Begin in Mountain. Inhale as you step back with your left foot.
2. Exhale as you bend forward, and place your right finger tips on the floor about 12 inches in front of your right toes. At the same time, lift your left leg into the air, keeping it straight and full of energy.

3. Inhale, placing your left hand on your left hip as you open your chest and hips to the side. You should feel like your entire body is facing the side wall, not the floor.

4. Exhale and slowly take your gaze to the side. (Once you have practiced for a while, try reaching your left hand straight up to the sky.)

Feel the front of your chest stretch and expand.

5. Take five breaths. As you hold the posture, feel a lightness in your body, as if someone is lifting you up through your left leg and arm. Don't forget your breathing!

6. Inhale. Slightly bend your right knee as you lift your torso up and lower your left foot to the floor.

7. Exhale and return to Mountain.

8. Repeat the steps on the other side, lifting your right leg.

Intense Side Stretch (Parsvottanasana)

Practice this posture to help soothe your body and cool your mind. The arm position helps release your shoulders and open your chest. This counteracts all the sitting and slumping we do during the day.

1. Begin in Mountain. Inhale and step back with your left foot, toes pointing forward.
2. Exhale, bringing your arms behind your back. Grab your elbows. (With practice you can press your palms together, fingers pointing up.)
3. Inhale as you look up and open your chest toward the sky. Lift your shoulders up and back.
4. Exhale and bend forward, leading with your chest.

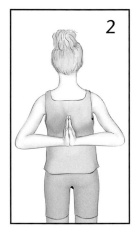

If this is difficult, grab your elbows instead.

5. Hold the posture for five breaths. Lengthen the front of your body to create a stretch from your tailbone to the top of your head. Keep lifting your shoulders and elbows up toward the sky. Gaze toward your toes.
6. Inhale as you come up slowly.
7. Exhale and release the posture. Stand in Mountain.
8. Repeat the sequence on the other side, with your right foot back.

At first, keep your back parallel to the floor. With practice, you will be able to lay your belly on your thigh and your nose on your shin.

What Are You Looking At?

Each posture has a traditional gazing point, or drishti. However, you can change the point that you look at. The most important thing is to keep your gaze on one point that you have chosen to look at. If your eyes wander around the room, looking at all different things, then you can't focus on what you're doing!

Tree (Vrikshasana)

Practicing Tree can help you feel calm and focused. Imagine yourself as a tall, graceful tree, with your feet rooted in the earth while your arms reach toward the sky like branches.

1. Stand in Mountain and root your feet in the ground. Keep the legs strong and steady.

2. Inhale as you shift your weight to the right foot and lift your left foot. Press the bottom of your left foot against the right inner thigh.

3. Exhale and bring your palms together in front of your chest. Keep your left knee pointing out to the side.

4. Inhale and raise your hands over your head, palms still pressing together.

Stand by a wall when you first start practicing. Use it to help you balance.

5. Hold the posture for five breaths. Gaze at one point in front of you to help you balance.
6. Exhale and slowly come back to Mountain.
7. Repeat on the other side.

Eagle (Garudasana)

The Eagle is a fun, yet challenging, balancing posture. It is named after a mythical eagle named Garuda, who had the body of a man and the beak and wings of an eagle.

1. Begin in Mountain.
2. Inhale as you bend your right knee slightly. Cross your left thigh over your right thigh. Hook your left toes behind your right calf. Reach your arms out to the sides.
3. Exhale and cross your right arm over your left arm, just above the elbows. Reach your palms toward each other.
4. Hold the posture for five breaths. Fix your gaze on a point past your hands. Gently squeeze your arms and legs together. Stand tall.
5. Inhale and slowly unwind from the posture, releasing your arms and legs.
6. Exhale and return to Mountain.
7. Repeat on the other side.

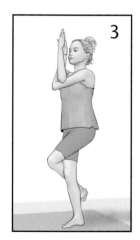

You can also practice the Eagle arms alone.

Intense West Stretch (Paschimottanasana)

Traditionally, yoga postures are practiced while facing the rising sun in the east. The back of the body faces the west. This posture stretches the back of the body, so it is called the Intense West Stretch. It stretches the back of the legs (the hamstring muscles) and the spine and back muscles. If you are just starting to learn yoga, you will need a cloth belt or strap for this posture.

1.   Sit down with your legs in front of you. Place the strap

on the floor by your feet. Inhale as you gently contract your thigh muscles. (You will see your kneecaps move toward you when you do this.) Keep your feet active by pulling the toes toward you. Gently pull your belly up and in. Reach your entire spine upward, sitting tall. Lift the shoulders up and back as you press your fingers into the floor by your hips.

2. Exhale. Fold forward, reaching your chest forward first and then reaching your arms out. Take hold of the strap, looping it around your feet. Keep your spine straight, folding forward from the hips (instead of bending at the waist). (Eventually, you can take hold of the big toes with your index and middle fingers. However, don't round your back in an effort to fold more. Keep your spine long, and use the strap until the backs of your legs have become more flexible.)

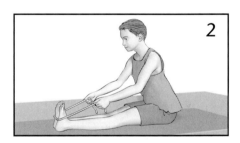

If you are having trouble folding forward, place a firm folded blanket just under your sitting bones.

3. Hold the posture for five breaths. Look to your toes. On each inhalation, lift and lengthen your spine a bit. On each exhalation, reach your chest toward your toes a bit. These are very small movements.

4. Inhale as you release your hold, and slowly lift yourself back to a sitting position.

Half Lord of the Fishes (Ardha Matsyendrasana)

It is said that Matsyendra, Lord of the Fishes, practiced and described this posture long ago, so it is named after him. This spinal twist helps you release tension in your upper back and shoulders. It can also stimulate the internal organs because you wring the torso like a wet towel and then you release it.

1. Inhale as you sit down with your legs reaching out in front of you.
2. Exhale and fold your left leg underneath your right leg so that the left heel sits next to your right hip. Bend your right knee so it points to the ceiling and the right foot presses into the floor next to your left knee.
3. Inhale. Press your sitting bones into the floor as you reach the top of your head up to the ceiling, sitting up tall. Reach your left arm up.
4. Exhale and twist to the right, bringing your left arm to the outside of your right knee. Turn your gaze over your right shoulder.

If your back starts to round, come out of the twist a little so you can sit tall and straight.

5. Hold the posture for five breaths. Use your inhalations to make your spine long and tall. Use your exhalations to help you twist farther.
6. Exhale and turn to face front. Release the posture slowly.
7. Repeat on the other side.

Bridge (Setu Bandhasana)

This posture strengthens and stretches the thighs. It also opens the front of the body, stretching the chest and abdomen. This opening and lifting of the upper body helps to balance all of the activities we do during the day—using computers, washing dishes, doing homework, and playing soccer—that require us to look down and lean forward.

1. Exhale as you lie on your back with your knees bent. Your knees and your feet should be hip-distance apart, with your feet underneath your knees. Your palms are pressing into the floor next to your hips.
2. Inhale. Slowly lift your hips off the floor, until you are resting on your shoulders and arms. Press your feet firmly into the floor. (The back of your neck should not touch the floor. The back of your head and your shoulders should touch the floor.)
3. Exhale and roll your shoulders underneath you as you interlock your fingers. Press your arms into the floor, and extend your chest to the sky.

4. Hold the posture for five breaths. Allow the inhalations to lift your chest and your hips higher. Make sure you feel no pain in your neck and lower back. (If you do, come out

Make sure your knees stay over your ankles. Do not let them fall out to the sides.

of the posture. You can try the posture again, but keep your palms pressing into the floor instead of interlocking your fingers.)

5. Exhale. Lower your hips back down to the floor and release your arms.

Camel (Ushtrasana)

Like Bridge, Camel stretches the front of the body. However, Camel is a more challenging posture, so take this one slowly.

1. Sit in a kneeling position. Lift your hips up off your heels so you are "standing" on your knees. Place the balls and toes of your feet on the floor. Place your hands on your hips.

2. Inhale and reach the top of your

Keep your legs and your abdomen strong as you lift your chest.

head and your chest up toward the sky as you slowly arch back from your upper back. Look toward the sky.

3. Exhale. If you feel good in this posture and want to go further, bring your hands back to rest on your heels.

4. Hold the posture for five breaths. When you inhale, lift the chest up to the sky. When you exhale, press your knees and feet into the floor. Look up toward the sky.

Try to keep your hips and thighs stretching forward.

5. Inhale, using your abdominal and thigh muscles to lift yourself back up to the kneeling position.

6. Exhale and sit back on your heels. Lean forward until your torso is lying on your thighs. If it's more comfortable, rest with your knees apart so your torso can fit in between the legs. Rest your forehead on the floor, and stretch your arms along the floor. Take as many breaths as you need.

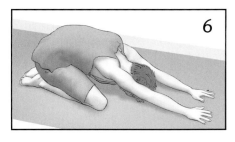

Let your body relax in this posture.

Classroom Yoga

Did you know that hundreds of schools across the United States are using yoga in their classrooms? Some schools include yoga as part of physical education class. Other schools have students practice yoga beside their desks during their academic classes. Still other schools have special rooms set aside just for practicing yoga.

Students say that practicing yoga helps them cope with the everyday stresses of school that come from classwork and social life. Teachers appreciate how a few yoga postures can help a class unwind after a big test and get ready to focus on learning something new. Student athletes find that practicing yoga helps them in their sport, both physically and mentally. Yoga helps them improve their flexibility, which helps prevent injuries during games, and it also helps to improve their concentration in a competition. And younger students find yoga to be just plain fun. There are even yoga games and songs that some teachers use to help kids remember and practice postures. Maybe you can talk to your physical education teacher about bringing yoga into your school!

Corpse (Shavasana)

At the end of your practice, it is important to spend five to twenty minutes in a resting posture. This lets you deepen the breath, clear the mind, and relax the entire body. It helps to first contract each part of your body before you let it completely relax onto the floor.

1. Lie on your back, and turn your palms open to the sky.

2. Inhale as you squeeze all the muscles in your face, scrunching it up and closing your eyes. Keeping your eyes closed, exhale and relax all those muscles.

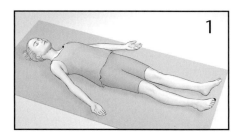

Relax every part of your body and turn your attention within.

3. Inhale and contract all the muscles in your shoulders, upper back, arms, and hands.

4. Exhale as you relax those muscles. Let the upper back and the arms sink into the floor.

5. Inhale, squeezing all the muscles in your abdomen, buttocks, and hips.

6. Exhale and relax them. Feel them sink into the ground.

7. Inhale as you contract all the muscles in your legs and feet.

8. Exhale and release them.

9. Once your body is relaxed, turn your attention completely within. Don't let sounds, smells, or anything else distract you. Stay completely still as you do this. To help you focus on your inner world, you can visualize a place that makes you happy. This may be an actual place that you have been, or it can be imaginary. It can be a wide-open field of green grass on a sunny day, or a favorite overstuffed chair, or a quiet pond where frogs call. Picture this place in your mind, and focus on it.

   If your mind starts to interfere by coming up with random thoughts—and it probably will—allow that to happen, but don't get attached to any of the thoughts. So if your mind says, "What's that sound?" or "I think I'm hungry," just let that thought float away. See if you can stay still for a set amount of time, for example, five minutes. You may

---

Now What Do I Do?

While you're in a posture

- *Look toward the gazing point (the drishti) for that posture.*
- *Listen to your breath.*
- *Focus your mind on what you are doing.*
- *Make small adjustments to the posture as you breathe. On the inhalations make your spine long. On the exhalations move farther into the posture.*

want to set an alarm. Stay awake and relaxed, not moving. This will become easier over time.

Other Yoga Postures

There are hundreds of yoga postures. Find a class or a book from the Further Resources section to learn more postures, including some that turn you upside down, such as a headstand and a handstand!

During your practice, remember that yoga is not competitive. Never force your body into a posture. Ease yourself gently into each position. When you are holding a pose, check to see if you can feel tension building up anywhere. If you do, focus on relaxing that tension using your breathing. Over time, your body will become more flexible and stronger.

Once you are familiar with the Sun Salutation and the postures we've described, you can link them together. Moving from one posture to another while focusing on each breath and linking it to the movement of the body is called *vinyasa* in Sanskrit. This can be a very powerful way to practice the yoga postures. Instead of resting or fidgeting after a posture, you just move right into the next one on the next breath. The postures we have described in this chapter can be practiced in this way, in the order in which you read them.

Practicing Pranayama

Did you realize that you take around 20,000 to 30,000 breaths each day? When was the last time you paid attention to even one of those breaths? Practicing pranayama helps us pay attention to our breath. We listen to it, feel it, and try different ways of working with it. By focusing on our breath, we can give the body energy, help reduce stress, and clear the mind so that we can concentrate and feel better.

Pranayama is a Sanskrit word made up of two words: prana, which means "life energy," and ayama, which means "to extend." Think of the breath coming into your body as this life energy, or prana. When we practice pranayama we are consciously bringing more of this prana into our body.

Abdominal Breathing

You can use abdominal breathing to help you relax, especially after a stressful day at school. When you practice this pranayama exercise, lie in Corpse (page 45) in a quiet place.

1. Place one hand on your belly button, just below your rib cage.
2. Close your eyes, and start to pay attention to

your breath. Breathe in and out through your nose, with your mouth shut. Notice the sound of your breath. Try to breathe naturally, and pay attention to how fast or slow you breathe in and out.

3. Slowly inhale enough to fill your lungs. This breath should make your belly move up a little, expanding. (Don't push your belly up; just relax it so it moves as you breathe.) If you open your eyes as you breathe in, you should see the hand on your belly rise. Then exhale, and let your belly fall. Continue to breathe, and pay attention to the area under your hand as it rises and falls.

Try abdominal breathing for one to five minutes. Then see how you feel. Are you more calm? Are you energized? Once you get used to breathing this way, you don't need to lie down. You can practice it anytime you need to calm down.

Once you have tried abdominal breathing and you can easily feel your belly rise and fall, you can start to notice how your breath moves other parts of your body, too. Keep your body relaxed in Corpse. Can you feel your back pressing a little into the floor as you inhale, and moving away from the floor as you exhale? What other parts of your torso can you feel moving as you breathe?

Three

Yoga Ways of Living

Yoga has a set of guidelines for how to live. These guidelines, the yama and niyama, are the first two limbs of Patanjali's eight-limbed path (refer to page 9 to see all eight limbs). Traditionally, people who became students of yoga masters began by following the yama and niyama to perfect their behavior. Today, however, many people start on the yoga path with asana, the postures we discussed in Chapter Two. After they realize how good they feel from practicing the postures, they start to learn about the other limbs.

The first set of guidelines, called the yama, describes ways to behave toward people and the environment: Don't do harm; don't lie; don't steal; don't waste energy; and don't be greedy. The second set of guidelines is the niyama, and those relate to how we treat ourselves. They include cleanliness, contentment, self-discipline, self-study, and surrender to the spirit in all of us.

Yama

The yama may sound like a lot of don'ts, but they have a positive purpose: to help us live peacefully with each other. These guidelines are just as important now as they were when Patanjali wrote them down two thousand years ago. In fact, you have probably heard some of these guidelines expressed in other ways at home or in school.

Don't Do Harm (Ahimsa)

Ahimsa, the first guideline, means "don't do harm." Some yogis call this practicing nonviolence. Violence is anything that causes pain. We all know that actions can cause pain, but words can cause pain, as well. Even

The practice of yoga teaches you the self-confidence and strength that allows you to be kinder to yourself, to other people, and to other living beings.

thoughts can cause pain. If you look in a mirror and think, *What awful legs,* or *These arms are so scrawny,* you are hurting yourself, as surely as you would hurt a friend if you said that to him or her. The practice of yoga teaches you the self-confidence and strength that allows you to be kinder to yourself, to other people, and to other living beings.

Get Connected

Yoga teaches that everything in the world is connected. For example, in science class you learn that a plant affects the soil while it lives, and when it dies, it becomes the soil as it breaks down. That plant affects other parts of the ecosystem, as well—it provides pollen for bees, and its leaves are eaten by insects, which are then eaten by birds... and so on.

In the same way, the choices we make in our lives affect the entire world. Some choices may be easy: Throw out that magazine or recycle it? Others may be more difficult: Fight with someone who has called you a name, or make a joke and laugh about it? If you start by feeling compassion and love for yourself, then you will be able to treat others with compassion and love, too.

Don't Lie (Satya)
The second yama is satya—not lying. Yoga encourages

you to be truthful with yourself and other people. It's no accident that "don't hurt" and "don't lie" are side by side here. Telling the truth must go hand in hand with being sensitive to how you say things to people, so you don't hurt them. If your best friend asks you why you can't hang out after school, and it's because you have plans with other friends, there are lots of ways to say this. Saying "I'm bored with playing video games at your house" will hurt your friend. Saying "Chris asked me over today. Let's do something Friday..." is being truthful without hurting anyone.

Don't Steal (Asteya)

The third guideline is asteya, not stealing. This one seems simple: Don't take what does not belong to you. However, this teaching goes beyond money or other material things. It also means don't steal other people's ideas, and don't take up people's time or energy unnecessarily. If you pursue honest ways of getting what you need, people will trust you. This trust will help you get what you need.

Don't Waste Energy (Brahmacharya)

The practice of brahmacharya encourages you to use your energy wisely. This means deciding carefully how you will spend your time and with whom you will spend it. When you spend time with friends, do you talk about things that really matter to you? Do you come home feeling good and energized?

If you're doing things like vandalizing property or drinking, then you're putting your energy into things that are destructive to yourself and others. Even just watching television for big chunks of time drains your energy. Find things that challenge you, that make you think and move in different ways and notice new things. This may mean finding new friends, joining a rock-climbing club, or going to the public library. When you find activities that make you feel good both *while* you're doing them and *after* you do them, you will start to notice that you don't need those old habits.

Don't Be Greedy (Aparigraha)

The final yama is aparigraha, not being greedy. Constantly wanting things that other people have is unhealthy. Material things do not help you figure out who you are, or what you want to do, or what you think is important. In fact, accumulating stuff can actually take up time and energy that you'd rather spend doing something else. Start to enjoy what you already have! This includes not just the things you have, but also the friends and family you have—even when they are not always what you think they "should" be.

> ## Yama for a Day
> *Want to try out the yama for yourself? Choose one of the yama: don't do harm; don't lie; don't steal; don't waste energy; or don't be greedy. For one day, follow that guideline as closely as you can. Remind yourself throughout the day to stick to it!*

Niyama

Besides the five yama, which show us how to exist in the world with others, there are also five niyama, which are guidelines for how to treat ourselves. The niyama are cleanliness, contentment, self-discipline, self-study, and surrender to the spirit in all of us.

Cleanliness (Saucha)

If you have ever taken a physically demanding yoga class with fifty other people, you'll understand why cleanliness is important! Early yoga teachers, although they probably worked with only one student at a time, no doubt felt the same way.

Cleanliness and purity extend to the inside of the body, as well. The practice of yoga encourages you to become more aware of what you eat and drink and how it affects your body. When you eat cookies or chips after school, how do you feel? When you drink a fruit smoothie that you made, how do you feel? You will start to notice the difference.

Contentment (Santosha)

The second niyama goes hand in hand with not being greedy. The practice of yoga shows you how to appreciate all that you have *and* be comfortable with what you do not have. Is there anyone who is content all the time? Probably not. Everyone has experiences that are painful or bothersome, but contentment is a way of responding to things that are out of your control by focusing on what you already have to be thankful about.

Self-discipline (Tapas)

The third niyama—tapas—is translated in many different ways, sometimes as "self-discipline" and "burning enthusiasm." Basically, it means "work hard." Many yogis practice tapas when they practice yoga postures. Others practice tapas by making dietary changes—they may give up caffeine or stop eating meat. Other yogis consider everything they do to be their tapas, putting their best effort, enthusiasm, and passion into every action they take.

Other yogis consider everything they do to be their tapas, putting their best effort, enthusiasm, and passion into every action they take.

Self-study (Svadhyaya)

This is one of the most important guidelines in yoga. When you practice yoga, you have time to focus entirely on yourself. You can observe how you feel when you try a challenging posture. Do you get angry? Sad? These observations can tell you about yourself. You can do this when you are with friends, parents, and teachers, too. Watch what you do. Think about why you do it and what it shows you about yourself.

Surrender to the Spirit (Ishvara Pranidhana)

The final guideline in yoga suggests that we surrender to the spirit in all of us. The idea of "surrender" is important. The guideline of "self-discipline" tells us to put our best effort into everything we do—but not everything is under our control! So how can we avoid being disappointed if we put all our effort into studying, but still get a C– on a test, or if we practice all year but don't make the team? At the same time that we put in our best effort, we let go of all our expectations of how things will turn out—we surrender to what will happen, now that we have done our best.

Some yogis see the "spirit" as referring to the way we are all connected, as we mentioned at the beginning of this chapter. They dedicate all their efforts to the good of all living beings. Others understand it to mean acknowledging the power of the divine. Yoga is not a religion itself, but some people find that in their yoga and meditation practices, they come to a deeper understanding of their religious faith.

Four

Yoga Stillness

We have already looked at the first four limbs of yoga: yama, niyama, asana, and pranayama. These first four limbs tend to be easier to practice than the last four. They are more physical, and they involve the outside world. The last four limbs—pratyahara, dharana, dhyana, and samadhi—help you turn your attention inward.

Pratyahara

Many of the limbs can be experienced while you are in a posture. For example, when you are in a posture, you can focus on your breath and make it slower. You can turn your attention from the outside world and concentrate fully on what you are doing at that moment. This is called pratyahara, or withdrawing the senses.

You can do this in any posture, but you may have noticed that Corpse (page 45) is one of the best for this purpose. In Corpse you close your eyes and totally relax your body, so you are able to take your attention away from what you see, hear, smell, taste, and touch. This is what it means to withdraw the senses from the outside world, or to practice pratyahara.

Sometimes it is a challenge to stop yourself from paying attention to the outside world, especially when you hear the traffic outside or feel the slam of the door downstairs. But with practice, it will become easier to stop getting caught up in what's going on around you. You can begin to focus on your breath going in and going out.

Dharana

Sometimes when you have brought all your attention to your "inside" world, the mind starts throwing thoughts at you, trying to distract you. These thoughts can make you lose focus. If you can focus completely on your breath and let the mind slow down, you have entered a state of dharana, or concentration. You are concentrating completely on one thing for a brief period of time.

Yoga Space

Some of the benefits of taking a yoga class come from going to a place that you know will be relaxing. You can make a place like this for yourself at home, too. For example, you can take one corner of your bedroom and turn it into your yoga space. You can place your yoga mat, a nice towel, or a throw rug on the floor. You can put together a collage of your favorite images to hang on the walls. You can also display small objects that you find inspiring. These can be simple things: the shape of a shell or the color of a flower can help you to relax. Don't make the area too cluttered, though—it should be easy to get to whenever you want to practice.

You may already know what dharana feels like. If you have ever found yourself absorbed completely in one thing, like practicing in a batting cage or singing a song, that's concentration. Maybe it has happened to you while you were working on a math problem or writing an essay. Once you got going, you became so involved in what you were doing that when you were done, you couldn't believe how much time had passed. That's concentration, too.

During yogic concentration you can choose anything to focus on. (On page 46, we've suggested that you focus

There's No Place Like Om

"Om" looks like a simple enough word. It's made up of only two letters, so how complicated could it be, right? In fact, yogis consider om to be the most sacred syllable a person can pronounce. According to ancient texts, om is the most basic sound and the sound of the universe. What does that mean? One way to think of it is to picture our universe as a giant drum. If you were to strike our universe like a drum, the vibrations from that strike would make the sound om. At the same time, if you could hear the tiniest atom as it vibrated, it would also produce the sound om.

Even though om has only two letters, it is made up of four sounds: A, U, M, and a final vibration or hum. You can practice saying om. Start by taking a nice deep breath in and making an ahhhh sound (A), as if you were saying "ah" for a doctor, with your mouth wide open. The sound is placed mostly toward the back of your mouth, in your throat. Then keep the sound going but change to the ohhhh sound (U). The sound moves from the back of your throat to the middle of your mouth, as if it's vibrating against the roof of your mouth. Now close your lips to make the mmmm sound (M), and the sound seems to move to the front of your mouth. Finally, let the hum of the mmmm move up into your nose, and slowly let the sound fade. Take another deep breath in, and try it again: ahhhhhhhhh-ohhhhhhhhh-mmmmmmmm .

People use the sound of om in many different ways. Sometimes it is used as a mantra. A mantra is a word, syllable, or phrase that is repeated over and over again in order to help focus the mind. Om is sometimes also chanted at the beginning or end of a yoga class. It brings together the voices of all the yoga students in the room. You may want to start or finish your yoga practice with om, as well.

on a place that makes you feel happy. You can also focus on the breath or on a sound like *Om*, discussed on pages 64-65.) Your concentration may be interrupted many times during one practice, and that's okay. What's important is that you come back to it. When you become aware that you have lost your concentration, bring it back to your original focus.

Dhyana

With practice, your concentration becomes so strong that it is no longer easily broken. This leads to uninterrupted concentration, or dhyana. This uninterrupted concentration is often called meditation. Meditation happens spontaneously and naturally. You cannot *make* yourself meditate; you can only make the effort to withdraw your senses and concentrate. When this concentration is intense enough and lasts long enough, then it will become meditation. There is no clear dividing line, but people experience different feelings as their practice develops and they move from concentration to meditation.

It is important to note that what you meditate on doesn't matter much—it can be anything. This makes sense because yoga teaches that *everything* is connected, so anything can inspire you. There are some things that are traditionally used for meditation. These include the breath, a feeling, certain sounds called mantras, and colorful designs called mandalas.

Samadhi

If meditation is intense enough and continues long enough, then it will move into samadhi. Samadhi is difficult to translate into English, but for many people who practice yoga, it's very important because it is the reason for practicing the other seven limbs of yoga.

At the beginning of Chapter 3 when we discussed ahimsa (nonviolence), we mentioned that yoga teaches that we are all connected. Samadhi is often explained as the state in which you *experience* that oneness and connectedness. In meditation (dhyana), the meditator focuses completely on one thing, like the breath, or a sound, or an object. However, he or she still sees him- or herself as separate from that thing. Yoga teaches that when dhyana becomes samadhi, the meditator experiences oneness with that thing. He or she *is* the breath, or the sound, or the object, and no longer sees any separation. Yoga teachings say that with samadhi comes a sense of bliss and joy.

Your Yoga Practice

You may decide to practice just one limb of yoga,

doing the postures each afternoon. Or you may decide to practice the postures and the guidelines for living. Or you may decide to try them all. Whatever form your yoga practice takes, you will discover new things about yourself and about yoga every day! Enjoy this wonderful gift that has been handed down through the ages and has taken so many new forms around the world today. Namaste.

Namaste

Namaste [na-mas-TEY] is a Sanskrit word that means "The light in me bows to (or salutes, or honors) the light in you." It is often said in greeting someone or when parting. At the end of a yoga class, the teacher will say "Namaste," not only to say good-bye but also as a way to thank and acknowledge the students for their efforts. The students respond by saying "Namaste" as well, to thank their teacher.

Glossary

Yogic Terms

ahimsa: nonviolence; not harming in action, word, or thought

aparigraha: not being greedy

asana: postures and movements of the body

asteya: not stealing

brahmacharya: using energy wisely

dharana: concentrating on one object, sound, feeling, or idea

dhyana: keeping concentration focused without interruption; meditation drishti: gazing point

ishvara-pranidhana: offering all that you do to the shared spirit

mantra: a sound that is repeated during concentration and meditation

niyama: guidelines for how to treat ourselves

om: the universal mantra; the sound the universe makes

prana: life energy

pranayama: breathing exercises; controlling the breath

pratyahara: withdrawing the senses from the outside world and looking within yourself

samadhi: absorption; connectedness

santosha: contentment; being happy with what you have

satya: truth-telling; not lying

saucha: cleanliness of the body and the environment

svadhyaya: studying the self in many ways

tapas: working hard; self-discipline with enthusiasm

ujjayi: a special way of breathing that can be done by itself or during yoga postures

vinyasa: linking movement and breath; flowing from one posture to another

yama: guidelines for how to live in the world with others

yogi: person who practices yoga, especially an advanced practitioner

Anatomical Terms

cardiovascular: Cardiovascular endurance has to do with how efficiently the heart and blood vessels work.

hip-distance: This is the distance between the bones that you can feel in the front of your hips. Place your hands on the sides of your waist, fingers in front. Find the bony parts of the pelvis that stick out in the front of your hips, just under your fingertips. Line up the second toe on each foot with the bones under your fingertips. Now your feet are hip-distance apart.

shoulder-distance: This is the distance between your shoulders. If you place your hands on the floor so that they are directly in line with your shoulders, your hands will be shoulder-distance apart.

sitting bones: These bones are technically called the ischial tuberosities. Sit on the edge of a hard chair, sitting up tall. Feel those two bones on the underside of your buttocks pressing down into the chair? Those are your sitting bones.

tailbone: This is the lowest part of the spine, and it is technically called the coccyx. Place one hand on your lower back to feel your spine. Follow the spine down to its base. That's your tailbone.

further Resources

Go to your local library to see what books, videos, audio-tapes, or compact discs they have. Some of the most helpful are listed below.

Books

Yoga Movement and Breath

Farhi, Donna. *Yoga Mind, Body, and Spirit: A Return to Wholeness*. New York: Henry Holt and Company, 2000.

Iyengar, B.K.S. *Yoga: The Path to Holistic Health*. London: DK Publishing, 2001.

Komitor, Jodi B. and Eve Adamson. *Complete Idiot's Guide to Yoga with Kids*. Alpha Books, 2000.

Luby, Thia. *Yoga for Teens: How to Improve Your Fitness, Confidence, Appearance, and Health—And Have Fun Doing It!* Santa Fe: Clear Light, 1999.

Swenson, David. *Ashtanga Yoga: The Practice Manual*. Houston, TX: Ashtanga Yoga Productions, 1999.

Trivell, Lisa. *I Can't Believe It's Yoga for Kids*. Long Island City: Hatherleigh, 2000.

Weiss, Stefanie Iris. *Everything You Need to Know About Yoga: An Introduction for Teens*. New York: Rosen Publishing Group, 1999.

Yoga Ways of Living

Satchidananda, Sri Swami. *The Yoga Sutras of Patanjali*. Buckingham, VA: Integral Yoga Publications, 1990.

Yoga Stillness

Gordhamer, Soren. *Just Say Om: Your Life's Journey*. Avon, MA: Adams Media Corporation, 2001.

Videotapes

Kalish, Leah. *Yoga Fitness For Kids Ages 7–12*, Broomfield, CO: Gaiam Americas.

Swenson, David. *Ashtanga Yoga: First Series*. Videotape, audiotape, or compact disc.

Yogamazing's Yoga for the Kid in All of Us, Roseland, NJ: Peter Pan Industries.

Web sites

www.anusara.com
www.ashtanga.com
www.iyengaryoga.com
www.jivamuktiyoga.com
www.kripalu.org
www.sivananda.org

Yoga classes

Look in the yellow pages of the phone book under YOGA or HEALTH CLUBS. If you don't see any, find the closest health-food store or independent bookstore and ask if they know of any yoga studios or classes. Also, these Web sites have directories of teachers and studios that can help find a yoga class near you:

www.yogajournal.com
www.yogadirectory.com
www.yogasite.com

You can also ask your physical education teachers to include yoga in physical education classes. This Web site for the Yoga on the Inside Foundation has information that can help a teacher start a yoga program in your school: www.yogainside.org/who/school.html.

Index

Pages in *italics* indicate illustrations.

About the Authors

Elizabeth Silas is a certified Ashtanga Vinyasa and Jivamukti yoga teacher whose teaching and practice draw on many forms of hatha yoga, including Anusara, Jivamukti, and Meridian Flexibility. She teaches yoga in Cincinnati and Oxford, Ohio, to adults and students. She has developed, written, and edited books for middle- and high-school students.

Diane Goodney is a music, language arts, and social studies teacher at a private school in Oxford, Ohio. She teaches yoga to her kindergarten through eighth grade students at school, as well as to adults in the community. She is certified in Ashtanga Vinyasa yoga but incorporates several forms of hatha yoga in her practice and instruction.

Acknowledgements

Our thanks go to Meredith DeSousa, our patient and thorough editor; Irena Miller, who provided an insightful review of the manuscript; and the many students of McGuffey Foundation School who have practiced yoga with us. From the bottom of our hearts, loving thanks to Patrick Baker and Tom Goodney for their encouragement and support.